Navigating Homosexualism in the Muslim World: Legal Challenges

Copyright Page

TITLE: Navigating Homosexualism in the Muslim World: Legal Challenges

1ST Edition

ISBN: 9798223163565

Table of Contents

Navigating Homosexualism in the Muslim World: Legal Challenges

By Roberto Miguel Rodriguez

Chapter 1: Introduction to Homosexualism in the Muslim World

Overview of Homosexualism in the Muslim World

Homosexuality remains a highly sensitive and controversial topic in the Muslim world, where cultural, religious, and legal norms often clash with the rights and identities of LGBTQ+ individuals. This subchapter aims to provide an overview of the challenges faced by LGBTQ+ Muslims, legal implications, advocacy efforts, and the experiences of LGBTQ+ individuals navigating their identities within Muslim communities.

The intersection of homosexuality and Islam has historically been contentious, with many interpretations of Islamic texts condemning same-sex relationships. This subchapter will explore the religious, cultural, and social factors that contribute to the stigmatization and marginalization of LGBTQ+ individuals in Muslim-majority countries.

Legal challenges faced by LGBTQ+ individuals in the Muslim world will be examined, including the criminalization of homosexuality in some jurisdictions and the impact of these laws on the lives of LGBTQ+ Muslims. It will also highlight the efforts of international attorneys and human rights organizations in advocating for LGBTQ+ rights in Muslim communities, while respecting the religious and cultural sensitivities.

The subchapter will shed light on the unique experiences of LGBTQ+ Muslims, exploring the dilemmas they face when reconciling their sexual orientation or gender identity with their faith. It will address the complexities of intersectionality, emphasizing the additional challenges faced by LGBTQ+ Muslims who are also members of other marginalized identities, such as race, ethnicity, or disability.

The subchapter will delve into the experiences of LGBTQ+ Muslim youth, covering topics such as coming out, family acceptance, and the need for support networks within their communities. It will also explore the representation and visibility of LGBTQ+ Muslims in media and arts, analyzing the role of positive portrayals in challenging stereotypes and promoting acceptance.

Furthermore, the subchapter will discuss LGBTQ+ Muslim activism and organizing, highlighting the efforts of individuals and organizations advocating for equal rights, social acceptance, and inclusive interpretations of Islam. It will also explore the emerging field of queer theology and its potential to reconcile LGBTQ+ identities with Islamic beliefs.

Lastly, the subchapter will examine the experiences of LGBTQ+ Muslim refugees, asylum seekers, and diaspora communities, considering the unique challenges they face as they navigate their identities in new cultural and legal contexts.

In conclusion, this subchapter provides an overview of the complex and multifaceted issues surrounding homosexuality in the Muslim world. It aims to inform international attorneys about the legal challenges faced by LGBTQ+ Muslims, the advocacy efforts being made, and the unique experiences and needs of LGBTQ+ individuals within Muslim communities. By understanding these issues, attorneys can better support and advocate for the rights and well-being of LGBTQ+ Muslims.

Historical Context and Cultural Perspectives

Understanding the historical context and cultural perspectives surrounding homosexuality in the Muslim world is crucial for international attorneys working in the areas of LGBTQ+ rights advocacy, legal challenges, and support networks for LGBTQ+

Muslims. This subchapter provides a comprehensive overview of the historical, cultural, and religious factors that shape the experiences of LGBTQ+ individuals living in Muslim-majority countries and communities.

The historical context reveals that diverse interpretations of Islamic teachings have existed throughout history, with attitudes towards homosexuality varying across time and geography. While same-sex relationships were once accepted and even celebrated in some Muslim societies, the influence of colonialism, Western norms, and conservative religious interpretations have contributed to the stigmatization and criminalization of homosexuality in many Muslim-majority countries.

Cultural perspectives towards homosexuality also differ within Muslim communities. Some societies maintain a more conservative outlook, viewing homosexuality as a deviation from traditional gender norms and religious teachings. Others, however, embrace more inclusive and progressive attitudes, recognizing the rights and dignity of LGBTQ+ individuals.

This subchapter delves into the challenges and experiences faced by LGBTQ+ Muslims, highlighting the intersections of their sexual orientation or gender identity with other marginalized identities such as race, ethnicity, and socio-economic status. It explores the unique struggles and discrimination faced by LGBTQ+ Muslim youth when coming out to their families and communities, and the potential consequences they may face, including rejection, violence, or even forced marriages.

The chapter also emphasizes the importance of support networks for LGBTQ+ Muslims, both within their faith communities and through LGBTQ+ organizations. These networks provide essential resources, safe spaces, and emotional support for individuals navigating the complexities of their sexual orientation or gender identity within a Muslim context.

Furthermore, the subchapter addresses the representation and visibility of LGBTQ+ Muslims in media and arts, highlighting the contribution of queer Muslim artists, activists, and scholars in challenging stereotypes and promoting acceptance and understanding.

Lastly, it explores the activism and organizing efforts of LGBTQ+ Muslims, showcasing the strategies employed to advocate for legal reform, social change, and greater inclusivity within their communities.

Overall, this subchapter offers international attorneys a comprehensive understanding of the historical context and cultural perspectives surrounding homosexuality in the Muslim world. By delving into the challenges, experiences, and activism of LGBTQ+ Muslims, it equips legal professionals with the necessary knowledge to navigate the complex legal landscape and advocate for the rights and dignity of LGBTQ+ individuals in Muslim communities globally.

Legal Frameworks and Challenges

In the complex and diverse landscape of the Muslim world, navigating the legal frameworks surrounding homosexualism presents numerous challenges. This subchapter explores the legal challenges faced by LGBTQ+ individuals in Muslim-majority countries and the advocacy efforts aimed at promoting their rights and well-being.

The legal landscape for homosexualism in the Muslim world varies greatly, with some countries criminalizing same-sex relationships, while others remain silent on the issue. These legal frameworks have profound consequences for LGBTQ+ individuals, who often face discrimination, harassment, and even violence due to their sexual orientation or gender identity.

One of the primary challenges faced by LGBTQ+ individuals in the Muslim world is the criminalization of same-sex relationships. Many countries enforce strict laws that punish consensual same-sex acts, ranging from imprisonment to even death. These laws not only violate fundamental human rights but also perpetuate a culture of fear and secrecy, forcing LGBTQ+ individuals to live in the shadows.

Advocacy for LGBTQ+ rights in Muslim communities faces unique challenges due to cultural and religious sensitivities. Balancing the promotion of LGBTQ+ rights with respect for religious beliefs and traditions requires a delicate approach. International attorneys involved in LGBTQ+ rights advocacy must navigate these complexities, engaging with religious scholars, community leaders, and legal experts to find common ground and promote understanding.

Intersectionality plays a crucial role in understanding the challenges faced by LGBTQ+ Muslims. LGBTQ+ individuals who belong to other marginalized identities, such as being a woman, a person of color, or a refugee, face compounded discrimination. Recognizing and addressing these intersecting identities is essential for effective advocacy and legal reform.

Support networks and safe spaces for LGBTQ+ Muslims are vital for their well-being and empowerment. These networks provide social, emotional, and legal support, creating spaces where individuals can express their authentic selves without fear of judgment or persecution. International attorneys can play a critical role in establishing and strengthening these networks, ensuring that LGBTQ+ Muslims have access to the resources they need.

Representation and visibility of LGBTQ+ Muslims in media and arts are crucial for challenging stereotypes and fostering acceptance. By amplifying the voices and experiences of LGBTQ+ Muslims, media and arts contribute to changing societal attitudes and challenging discriminatory laws and practices.

LGBTQ+ Muslim activism and organizing are essential drivers of change. This subchapter explores the various forms of activism and organizing undertaken by LGBTQ+ Muslims and their allies, ranging from grassroots movements to transnational advocacy networks. International attorneys can support these efforts by providing legal expertise, resources, and advocacy at both local and international levels.

Queer theology and interpretations of Islam offer alternative narratives that challenge traditional interpretations that condemn homosexuality. By examining religious texts and engaging in theological debates, LGBTQ+ individuals and their allies seek to reconcile their faith with their sexual orientation or gender identity, providing new perspectives that promote acceptance and inclusion.

The plight of LGBTQ+ Muslim refugees and asylum seekers highlights the need for legal protections and support. Fleeing persecution in their home countries, these individuals face additional challenges as they seek safety and acceptance in new societies. International attorneys can play a vital role in advocating for their rights and ensuring their access to legal protection.

Finally, LGBTQ+ Muslim diaspora communities face unique experiences and challenges in navigating both their religious and sexual identities. This subchapter explores the intersection of these identities and the ways in which LGBTQ+ Muslim diaspora communities carve out spaces for themselves while challenging cultural norms and promoting acceptance and understanding.

By examining the legal frameworks and challenges surrounding homosexualism in the Muslim world, this subchapter aims to provide international attorneys with a comprehensive understanding of the issues at hand. Through legal advocacy, engagement with religious scholars and community leaders, and support for LGBTQ+ individuals and communities, international attorneys can contribute to the advancement of LGBTQ+ rights in Muslim-majority countries and beyond.

Chapter 2: LGBTQ+ Rights Advocacy in Muslim Communities

Importance of Advocacy for LGBTQ+ Rights

The Importance of Advocacy for LGBTQ+ Rights

In recent years, the global conversation surrounding LGBTQ+ rights has gained tremendous momentum. While progress has been made in some parts of the world, the Muslim community continues to face unique challenges in navigating the intersection of homosexuality and religious beliefs. This subchapter aims to shed light on the importance of advocacy for LGBTQ+ rights within the Muslim world, providing international attorneys with valuable insights into the legal challenges and advocacy strategies needed to support this marginalized group.

Homosexualism in the Muslim World is a complex and sensitive issue that demands our attention. LGBTQ+ individuals within Muslim communities often face discrimination, stigmatization, and even persecution. It is essential for international attorneys to understand the legal framework surrounding homosexuality in Muslim-majority countries and the cultural and religious factors that shape attitudes towards LGBTQ+ individuals. By familiarizing themselves with these dynamics, attorneys can better advocate for the rights of LGBTQ+ Muslims.

Challenges and Experiences of LGBTQ+ Muslims are often multifaceted. These individuals may struggle with internal conflicts between their sexual orientation and their faith, which can lead to mental health issues and self-acceptance challenges. International attorneys should be equipped with the necessary knowledge and resources to support LGBTQ+ Muslims through legal avenues, providing them with the means to fight against discrimination and secure their rights.

Intersectionality is a crucial aspect of LGBTQ+ rights advocacy in Muslim communities. LGBTQ+ Muslims often face overlapping forms of discrimination based on their sexual orientation, gender identity, race, or socioeconomic status. It is imperative for international attorneys to understand these intersecting identities and their impact on the experiences and needs of LGBTQ+ Muslims. By adopting an intersectional approach, attorneys can better address the specific challenges faced by this community.

Representation and visibility of LGBTQ+ Muslims in media and arts play a significant role in challenging stereotypes and fostering acceptance. International attorneys can contribute to this cause by promoting inclusive narratives and supporting LGBTQ+ Muslim artists and media creators. By amplifying their voices, attorneys can help reshape public perceptions and create a more inclusive environment for LGBTQ+ Muslims.

Advocacy efforts should also extend to supporting LGBTQ+ Muslim refugees and asylum seekers. These individuals often face additional challenges due to their dual status as religious minorities and sexual minorities. International attorneys can play a pivotal role in ensuring their safety, providing legal guidance, and advocating for inclusive refugee and asylum policies.

Finally, LGBTQ+ Muslim diaspora communities deserve attention and support. International attorneys can collaborate with grassroots organizations and community leaders to create safe spaces, offer legal assistance, and promote dialogue on LGBTQ+ issues within these communities.

In conclusion, the importance of advocacy for LGBTQ+ rights in the Muslim world cannot be overstated. International attorneys have a vital role to play in navigating the legal challenges and advocating for the rights of LGBTQ+ Muslims. By understanding the complexities of LGBTQ+ rights within the Muslim community, attorneys can provide effective legal support, challenge discrimination, and work towards a more inclusive society.

Strategies for Advocacy in Muslim Communities

Advocacy for LGBTQ+ rights in Muslim communities requires a nuanced and culturally sensitive approach. It is essential to understand the unique challenges faced by LGBTQ+ individuals within these communities and develop strategies that resonate with their cultural, religious, and social contexts. This subchapter explores effective strategies for advocacy in Muslim communities to promote LGBTQ+ rights and address the legal challenges faced by LGBTQ+ individuals in the Muslim world.

1. Cultural Competence: Advocates working in Muslim communities must possess a deep understanding of Islamic teachings, traditions, and cultural norms. This knowledge will enable them to engage in informed and respectful conversations with community members, promoting dialogue and understanding.

2. Collaborative Engagement: Building alliances with local organizations, community leaders, and religious scholars who are supportive of LGBTQ+ rights is crucial. These partnerships can help bridge the gap between LGBTQ+ individuals and the broader Muslim community, fostering acceptance and solidarity.

3. Education and Awareness: Advocacy efforts should focus on providing accurate information about sexual orientation and gender identity, dispelling myths, and challenging misconceptions. Educational

campaigns can be conducted through workshops, seminars, and online platforms to reach a wider audience.

4. Empowering LGBTQ+ Muslims: Advocates should prioritize empowering LGBTQ+ Muslims by providing them with the necessary resources, support networks, and safe spaces. Creating spaces for LGBTQ+ Muslims to share their experiences, offer guidance, and connect with others facing similar challenges can be immensely beneficial.

5. Legal Reforms: Advocacy efforts should aim to challenge discriminatory laws and policies that criminalize homosexuality or deny LGBTQ+ individuals their rights. Engaging with international human rights organizations, partnering with legal experts, and lobbying for legal reforms can help in this regard.

6. Media and Arts Representation: Advocates should work towards increasing the visibility and representation of LGBTQ+ Muslims in media and the arts. Promoting positive portrayals can challenge stereotypes, humanize LGBTQ+ individuals, and foster empathy and understanding within the broader Muslim community.

7. Intersectionality and Allyship: Recognizing the intersections of LGBTQ+ identity with other marginalized identities, such as race, gender, and class, is crucial. Advocacy efforts should aim to address the unique challenges faced by LGBTQ+ Muslims who belong to multiple marginalized communities, and encourage allyship among different groups.

By employing these strategies, advocates can effectively navigate the challenges of advocating for LGBTQ+ rights in Muslim communities. While progress may be gradual, the ultimate goal is to create inclusive and accepting spaces where LGBTQ+ individuals in the Muslim world can live their lives authentically, free from discrimination and persecution.

Case Studies of Successful Advocacy Efforts

Chapter 3: Challenges and Experiences of LGBTQ+ Muslims

Coming to Terms with One's Sexuality in a Muslim Environment

Introduction:

Navigating one's sexuality can be a challenging journey, particularly in a Muslim environment where cultural and religious norms often intersect. This subchapter will delve into the experiences and challenges faced by individuals who identify as LGBTQ+ in the Muslim world. It will explore the legal hurdles, advocacy efforts, and personal stories that shed light on the intersectionality of LGBTQ+ rights and Muslim communities.

Legal Challenges and Advocacy:

In many countries with a Muslim majority, laws criminalizing homosexuality persist, making it difficult for LGBTQ+ individuals to come to terms with their sexuality openly. This section will discuss the legal challenges faced by LGBTQ+ individuals in the Muslim world, focusing on the impact of these laws on their lives. It will also highlight the advocacy efforts undertaken by international attorneys to challenge discriminatory legislation and promote LGBTQ+ rights within Muslim communities.

Challenges and Experiences of LGBTQ+ Muslims:

Coming to terms with one's sexuality within a Muslim environment can be an arduous process, often accompanied by fear, guilt, and social ostracism. This section will explore the unique challenges faced by LGBTQ+ Muslims, including the clash between religious teachings and personal identity. It will provide personal narratives that shed light on the emotional and psychological struggles experienced by individuals grappling with their sexuality while adhering to their faith.

Intersectionality: LGBTQ+ Muslims and other marginalized identities:

Intersectionality plays a pivotal role when discussing the experiences of LGBTQ+ Muslims. This section will examine how LGBTQ+ Muslims navigate their identities in relation to other marginalized aspects of their lives, such as race, gender, and socio-economic status. It will emphasize the importance of acknowledging and addressing the multiple layers of discrimination faced by LGBTQ+ Muslims to foster a more inclusive and understanding society.

LGBTQ+ Muslim Youth and Coming Out:

Coming out is a significant milestone for many individuals, but it can be particularly challenging for LGBTQ+ Muslim youth. This section will shed light on the experiences of LGBTQ+ Muslim youth as they grapple with their sexuality, often in the face of familial expectations and cultural norms. It will explore the importance of creating safe spaces and support networks to aid LGBTQ+ Muslim youth in their journey towards self-acceptance and understanding.

Support Networks for LGBTQ+ Muslims:

In a Muslim environment where LGBTQ+ individuals may face isolation and rejection, support networks play a vital role. This section will discuss the various support systems available for LGBTQ+ Muslims, including LGBTQ+ organizations, faith-based communities, and online resources. It will emphasize the significance of fostering inclusive spaces that promote acceptance and provide a sense of belonging for LGBTQ+ Muslims.

Representation and Visibility of LGBTQ+ Muslims in Media and Arts:

Representation and visibility are powerful tools in challenging stereotypes and promoting acceptance. This section will explore the importance of LGBTQ+ Muslim representation in media and the arts. It will highlight the progress made in recent years and discuss the impact of LGBTQ+ Muslim stories in shaping public opinions and fostering dialogue within Muslim communities.

LGBTQ+ Muslim Activism and Organizing:

Activism and organizing are crucial in advocating for LGBTQ+ rights within Muslim communities. This section will delve into the efforts made by LGBTQ+ Muslim activists and organizations to challenge discriminatory laws and promote acceptance and understanding. It will highlight successful initiatives and discuss the strategies employed to effect change within cultural and religious frameworks.

Queer Theology and Interpretations of Islam:

This section will explore the concept of queer theology and its intersection with Islam. It will discuss alternative interpretations of Islamic teachings that embrace LGBTQ+ individuals and challenge traditional views. It will highlight the importance of fostering dialogue between religious scholars, LGBTQ+ Muslims, and the wider Muslim community to foster inclusive interpretations of Islam.

LGBTQ+ Muslim Refugees and Asylum Seekers:

LGBTQ+ Muslims fleeing persecution in their home countries often face unique challenges as refugees and asylum seekers. This section will shed light on their experiences, including the difficulties of navigating international legal systems, seeking asylum based on sexual orientation or gender identity, and finding safe spaces within host countries. It will also explore the support systems available for LGBTQ+ Muslim refugees and the need for more comprehensive protection mechanisms.

LGBTQ+ Muslim Diaspora Communities and Experiences:

The experiences of LGBTQ+ Muslims within diaspora communities present a unique set of challenges and opportunities. This section will explore the intersection of LGBTQ+ identities and cultural assimilation, the role of diaspora communities in providing support, and the efforts made to bridge gaps between LGBTQ+ Muslims and their cultural heritage. It will highlight the importance of fostering dialogue and understanding within diaspora communities to create inclusive spaces for LGBTQ+ individuals.

Conclusion:

Coming to terms with one's sexuality in a Muslim environment is a multifaceted journey, fraught with challenges and opportunities. This subchapter has explored the legal, personal, and cultural aspects of LGBTQ+ experiences in the Muslim world. By shedding light on these topics, it is hoped that international attorneys and advocates can better understand the unique challenges faced by LGBTQ+ individuals in Muslim communities and work towards promoting acceptance, inclusivity, and human rights for all.

Discrimination and Stigmatization Faced by LGBTQ+ Muslims

Introduction:

In the struggle for LGBTQ+ rights, Muslim communities face unique challenges due to the intersectionality of their identities. This subchapter explores the discrimination and stigmatization experienced by LGBTQ+ Muslims, shedding light on the legal, social, and cultural barriers they encounter within their communities and the broader Muslim world.

Legal Challenges:

LGBTQ+ Muslims often face legal hurdles in countries where homosexuality is criminalized under Sharia law. These laws not only perpetuate discrimination but also stigmatize and marginalize individuals based on their sexual orientation or gender identity. International attorneys can play a crucial role in challenging these laws and advocating for legal reforms to protect the rights of LGBTQ+ Muslims.

Social and Cultural Stigmatization:

Within Muslim communities, LGBTQ+ individuals face social and cultural stigmatization due to deeply-rooted conservative beliefs and societal norms. Homosexualism is often considered taboo, leading to ostracization, exclusion, and even violence against LGBTQ+ Muslims. The subchapter delves into the cultural dynamics that contribute to this stigmatization and offers insights on how international attorneys can engage with local communities to promote understanding and acceptance.

Intersectionality and Marginalization:

LGBTQ+ Muslims often experience intersecting forms of marginalization, including racism, sexism, and religious discrimination. This subchapter explores the unique challenges faced by LGBTQ+ Muslims in navigating their identities and highlights the importance of recognizing and addressing these intersecting forms of oppression in advocacy efforts.

Support Networks and Visibility:

Creating safe spaces and support networks for LGBTQ+ Muslims is crucial in combating discrimination and stigmatization. The subchapter examines the role of support organizations, both within Muslim communities and internationally, in providing resources, counseling, and community for LGBTQ+ Muslims. It also explores the importance of visibility and representation in media and the arts, challenging stereotypes and fostering understanding.

Conclusion:

Addressing the discrimination and stigmatization faced by LGBTQ+ Muslims requires a multi-faceted approach that combines legal advocacy, social engagement, and cultural change. International attorneys have a vital role to play in challenging discriminatory laws, promoting acceptance, and supporting LGBTQ+ Muslims in their journey towards equality and inclusion. By understanding the unique challenges faced by LGBTQ+ Muslims, attorneys can contribute to building a more inclusive and accepting world for all.

Mental Health Challenges and Support

Introduction:

In the realm of advocating for LGBTQ+ rights in Muslim communities, it is essential to address the mental health challenges faced by individuals navigating their sexual orientation or gender identity. This subchapter aims to explore the unique struggles experienced by LGBTQ+ Muslims and provide insights into the support systems available to them.

Understanding Mental Health Challenges:

LGBTQ+ Muslims often face a multitude of mental health challenges due to societal stigma, discrimination, and the conflicts between their sexual orientation or gender identity and their religious beliefs. These struggles can lead to increased rates of anxiety, depression, self-harm, and even suicidal ideation within this community.

Intersectionality: LGBTQ+ Muslims and Other Marginalized Identities:

Acknowledging the intersectionality of LGBTQ+ Muslims is crucial. Many individuals in this community also face additional marginalization based on race, ethnicity, socioeconomic status, disability, or immigration status. These intersecting identities further compound the mental health challenges faced by LGBTQ+ Muslims and require a comprehensive approach to support.

Support Networks for LGBTQ+ Muslims:

Creating a strong support network is vital for the mental well-being of LGBTQ+ Muslims. This subchapter will explore the existing support systems, both within and outside Muslim communities, which provide safe spaces for individuals to share their experiences, seek guidance, and find solace. It will highlight LGBTQ+ Muslim organizations, counseling services, and online platforms that offer support and resources to address mental health challenges.

LGBTQ+ Muslim Youth and Coming Out:

The coming-out process can be particularly challenging for LGBTQ+ Muslim youth, as it involves navigating their sexual orientation or gender identity within the context of their faith and family dynamics. This subchapter will discuss the unique mental health challenges faced by LGBTQ+ Muslim youth and explore strategies to support them during this pivotal phase of self-discovery.

Representation and Visibility of LGBTQ+ Muslims in Media and Arts:

Positive representation and visibility of LGBTQ+ Muslims in media and the arts play a crucial role in promoting acceptance and understanding. This section will delve into the power of storytelling, art, and media in challenging stereotypes and fostering empathy towards LGBTQ+ Muslims, ultimately contributing to improved mental health outcomes.

Conclusion:

Addressing mental health challenges is an essential aspect of advocating for LGBTQ+ rights in Muslim communities. By understanding the unique struggles faced by LGBTQ+ Muslims, promoting intersectionality, establishing support networks, nurturing LGBTQ+ Muslim youth, enhancing representation, and fostering acceptance, we can contribute to a healthier and more inclusive environment for all individuals navigating their sexual orientation or gender identity within the Muslim world.

Chapter 4: Intersectionality: LGBTQ+ Muslims and Other Marginalized Identities

Intersectionality and its Relevance to LGBTQ+ Muslims

In recent years, the concept of intersectionality has gained significant attention within the field of social justice and advocacy. It acknowledges that individuals can experience multiple forms of oppression and discrimination simultaneously, based on their intersecting identities such as race, gender, class, and sexuality. When it comes to LGBTQ+ Muslims, the notion of intersectionality becomes particularly important in understanding the unique challenges they face within their communities and the broader society.

For many LGBTQ+ Muslims, the struggle for acceptance and inclusion is twofold. On one hand, they must navigate the complexities of their sexual orientation or gender identity within Muslim communities that often adhere to traditional interpretations of Islam. On the other hand, they also face discrimination and marginalization within LGBTQ+ spaces that may not fully understand or respect their religious beliefs.

The intersectionality of being both LGBTQ+ and Muslim can lead to a multitude of challenges and experiences. LGBTQ+ Muslims may face rejection from their families, communities, and religious institutions, which can result in feelings of isolation and loneliness. They may also encounter difficulties in reconciling their faith with their sexual orientation or gender identity, often grappling with conflicting messages from religious teachings and societal norms.

Despite these challenges, LGBTQ+ Muslims have found ways to navigate their identities and create support networks within their communities. Organizations and individuals have emerged to provide resources, counseling, and safe spaces specifically tailored to the needs of LGBTQ+ Muslims. These support networks play a crucial role in providing a sense of belonging, understanding, and validation for LGBTQ+ Muslims who often feel caught between two worlds.

Representation and visibility of LGBTQ+ Muslims in media and arts have also been instrumental in challenging stereotypes and misconceptions. Through their stories, LGBTQ+ Muslims are able to humanize their experiences and shed light on the complexities of their identities. Additionally, activism and organizing by LGBTQ+ Muslims have been instrumental in advocating for their rights within both Muslim and LGBTQ+ communities.

Furthermore, queer theology and interpretations of Islam have emerged as a way to reconcile faith and sexual orientation or gender identity. These interpretations seek to provide alternative readings of religious texts that affirm the existence and worth of LGBTQ+ individuals within Islamic teachings.

The experiences of LGBTQ+ Muslim refugees and asylum seekers further highlight the importance of intersectionality. They face the additional challenges of displacement, cultural adaptation, language barriers, and limited access to resources and support. LGBTQ+ Muslim diaspora communities play a crucial role in providing a sense of belonging and understanding for these individuals, helping them navigate their identities in a foreign context.

In conclusion, intersectionality is a key lens through which to understand the challenges and experiences of LGBTQ+ Muslims. The unique intersection of their sexual orientation or gender identity with their religious beliefs shapes their lives in complex ways. By acknowledging and addressing the intersectional oppressions faced by LGBTQ+ Muslims, international attorneys can better advocate for their rights and contribute to the advancement of LGBTQ+ rights advocacy in Muslim communities worldwide.

Experiences of LGBTQ+ Muslims with Multiple Identities

Introduction:

In this subchapter, we will explore the experiences of LGBTQ+ Muslims who navigate multiple identities and the unique challenges they face. These individuals find themselves at the intersection of their sexual orientation or gender identity and their religious and cultural backgrounds, creating complex and often conflicting identities. Understanding and addressing these experiences is crucial for international attorneys working in the fields of Homosexualism in the Muslim World, LGBTQ+ Rights Advocacy in Muslim communities, and related areas.

Navigating Multiple Identities:

LGBTQ+ Muslims often find themselves torn between their faith and their sexual orientation or gender identity, which can lead to internal conflict and feelings of isolation. They may fear rejection from their families, communities, and religious institutions, facing the difficult task of reconciling their identities and seeking acceptance.

Intersectionality and Marginalization:

The experiences of LGBTQ+ Muslims are further complicated by the intersectionality of their identities. Many individuals face discrimination not only based on their sexual orientation or gender identity but also due to their race, ethnicity, socioeconomic status, or disability. These overlapping identities contribute to increased marginalization and limited access to resources and support networks.

LGBTQ+ Muslim Youth and Coming Out:

Coming out as LGBTQ+ is a significant challenge for Muslim youth, who often struggle with societal and familial expectations. They face the fear of rejection, abandonment, or even violence. The lack of visibility and representation of LGBTQ+ Muslims in media and arts exacerbates their feelings of isolation and can hinder their self-acceptance and understanding.

Support Networks and Activism:

Support networks play a crucial role in the lives of LGBTQ+ Muslims. These networks provide a safe space for individuals to share their experiences, seek advice, and find solace. LGBTQ+ Muslim activists and organizations have emerged globally, advocating for the rights and well-being of this marginalized group. Their work aims to challenge harmful stereotypes, bridge the gap between religious teachings and LGBTQ+ acceptance, and create inclusive spaces within Muslim communities.

Queer Theology and Interpretations of Islam:

Queer theology and alternative interpretations of Islamic teachings have gained traction within LGBTQ+ Muslim communities. By examining religious texts through a queer lens, individuals seek to find acceptance within their faith and promote inclusivity. These interpretations challenge traditional interpretations that often stigmatize LGBTQ+ individuals.

Refugees, Asylum Seekers, and Diaspora:

LGBTQ+ Muslims who flee their home countries due to persecution often face additional challenges as refugees or asylum seekers. They may encounter discrimination and hostility within host countries, adding another layer of complexity to their identities. LGBTQ+ Muslim diaspora communities have emerged, providing a sense of belonging and solidarity for those navigating multiple identities.

Conclusion:

The experiences of LGBTQ+ Muslims with multiple identities are multifaceted and require attention from international attorneys, advocates, and communities. Understanding the challenges they face, supporting their unique needs, and promoting inclusivity within Muslim communities are vital steps toward ensuring the rights and well-being of LGBTQ+ individuals worldwide. By addressing these issues, we can work towards a more inclusive and accepting future for all.

Building Solidarity and Support Networks

In the struggle for LGBTQ+ rights and acceptance, building solidarity and support networks is crucial. This subchapter explores the importance of these networks in the context of homosexuality in the Muslim world, and provides guidance for international attorneys seeking to advocate for change.

Homosexualism in the Muslim world is a complex and challenging topic, with legal and cultural barriers often hindering progress. However, by fostering solidarity among LGBTQ+ individuals, allies, and organizations, change can be achieved. This subchapter will outline the various ways in which international attorneys can contribute to this process.

One of the key areas of focus is LGBTQ+ rights advocacy in Muslim communities. By working with local NGOs, legal experts can provide valuable support and expertise to amplify the voices of LGBTQ+ individuals and challenge discriminatory laws. This involves understanding the unique challenges faced by LGBTQ+ Muslims and tailoring advocacy efforts to address these specific concerns.

A critical aspect of building solidarity is recognizing the intersectionality of LGBTQ+ Muslims and their experiences. This subchapter delves into the intersectionality of LGBTQ+ identities with other marginalized identities, such as race, gender, and religion. By acknowledging and addressing these multiple dimensions of oppression, attorneys can work towards more inclusive and effective advocacy strategies.

Support networks play a vital role in the lives of LGBTQ+ Muslims. This subchapter discusses the various forms of support that can be provided, including mental health resources, safe spaces, and peer support groups. It also explores the importance of representation and visibility of LGBTQ+ Muslims in media and the arts, as a means of fostering understanding and acceptance within Muslim communities.

LGBTQ+ Muslim activism and organizing are powerful tools for effecting change. Attorneys can play a crucial role in supporting these efforts, providing legal guidance, and advocating for the rights of LGBTQ+ Muslims at national and international levels.

The subchapter also examines queer theology and interpretations of Islam, exploring how progressive interpretations can challenge conservative views and promote inclusivity. It further addresses the unique challenges faced by LGBTQ+ Muslim refugees and asylum seekers, as well as the experiences of LGBTQ+ Muslim diaspora communities.

In conclusion, building solidarity and support networks is essential for advancing LGBTQ+ rights in the Muslim world. International attorneys have a significant role to play in this process, by advocating for change, supporting local organizations, and empowering LGBTQ+ Muslims to assert their rights and live authentically. By fostering unity and understanding, we can work towards a more inclusive and accepting future for all LGBTQ+ individuals, regardless of their religious or cultural background.

Chapter 5: LGBTQ+ Muslim Youth and Coming Out

Unique Challenges Faced by LGBTQ+ Muslim Youth

Chapter Title: Unique Challenges Faced by LGBTQ+ Muslim Youth

Subchapter: Unique Challenges Faced by LGBTQ+ Muslim Youth

Introduction:

LGBTQ+ Muslim youth face unique challenges within their communities due to the intersection of their sexual orientation or gender identity and their religious beliefs. This subchapter explores the various obstacles faced by these individuals, shedding light on their experiences and the need for advocacy and support within Muslim communities.

1. Cultural and Religious Stigma:

LGBTQ+ Muslim youth often struggle with the cultural and religious stigma attached to homosexuality or gender nonconformity. They may face condemnation, rejection, and even threats from their families, friends, and religious leaders. The clash between their sexual orientation or gender identity and religious teachings can lead to internal conflict and feelings of guilt or shame.

2. Coming Out and Acceptance:

Coming out as LGBTQ+ can be an incredibly challenging process for Muslim youth. Fear of rejection, isolation, or violence can hinder their ability to be open about their identities. They often grapple with the fear of losing their family, faith community, and social support systems, making the coming-out journey particularly difficult.

3. Lack of Support Networks:

LGBTQ+ Muslim youth often struggle to find safe spaces and support networks that understand their unique experiences. The lack of visibility and representation within Muslim communities results in limited resources and support systems. This isolation can lead to higher rates of mental health issues, including depression, anxiety, and suicidal ideation.

4. Intersectionality and Multiple Marginalized Identities:

LGBTQ+ Muslim youth may also face discrimination and marginalization based on other aspects of their identity, such as race, ethnicity, or socioeconomic status. The intersections of these identities can compound the challenges they face, further limiting their access to resources and support.

5. Balancing Faith and Identity:

Many LGBTQ+ Muslim youth strive to reconcile their faith with their sexual orientation or gender identity. They may seek alternative interpretations of Islamic teachings that affirm their identities or engage in queer theology. These individuals often face resistance from conservative religious authorities, making it difficult to find acceptance within their faith communities.

Conclusion:

The unique challenges faced by LGBTQ+ Muslim youth demand attention and action from international attorneys and advocates. By understanding these obstacles, legal professionals can work towards creating inclusive spaces, advocating for LGBTQ+ rights, and supporting the mental well-being of LGBTQ+ Muslim youth. This subchapter highlights the need for legal reforms, cultural sensitivity, and the creation of support networks within Muslim communities to address the challenges faced by these individuals.

Supportive Resources and Organizations for LGBTQ+ Muslim Youth

Introduction:

Navigating Homosexualism in the Muslim World: Legal Challenges and Advocacy aims to provide international attorneys with a comprehensive understanding of the unique challenges faced by LGBTQ+ individuals within Muslim communities. This subchapter focuses specifically on supportive resources and organizations available to LGBTQ+ Muslim youth. By highlighting these valuable support networks, we aim to empower attorneys to better advocate for the rights and well-being of this marginalized group.

1. The Muslim Alliance for Sexual and Gender Diversity (MASGD):

MASGD is a grassroots organization that provides a safe and inclusive space for LGBTQ+ Muslims. Their resources include support groups, online forums, and educational materials. The organization also hosts annual LGBTQ+ Muslim retreats to foster community building and personal growth.

2. LGBTQ+ Muslim Support Hotlines:

Several hotlines operate globally to provide immediate support and guidance to LGBTQ+ Muslim youth. These helplines offer confidential and non-judgmental counseling services and can be a lifeline for individuals facing isolation or discrimination.

3. LGBTQ+ Muslim Online Communities:

Online platforms such as social media groups and forums provide LGBTQ+ Muslim youth with a sense of belonging and connection. These communities allow individuals to share experiences, seek advice, and find support from others who understand their unique struggles.

4. LGBTQ+ Muslim Scholars and Activists:

Numerous LGBTQ+ Muslim scholars and activists are working to reconcile their faith and sexuality. Their writings, lectures, and advocacy efforts provide valuable resources for LGBTQ+ Muslim youth seeking to navigate their identities within the framework of Islam.

5. LGBTQ+ Inclusive Mosques and Islamic Centers:

A growing number of inclusive mosques and Islamic centers are emerging worldwide, providing LGBTQ+ Muslims with welcoming spaces to worship and engage with their religion. These organizations often host LGBTQ+ inclusive events, sermons, and discussions.

6. LGBTQ+ Muslim Youth Support Programs:

Various organizations offer specific programs aimed at supporting LGBTQ+ Muslim youth. These programs may include mentorship opportunities, mental health resources, and educational initiatives to promote self-acceptance and empower LGBTQ+ Muslim youth.

Conclusion:

Recognizing and promoting supportive resources and organizations for LGBTQ+ Muslim youth is crucial in addressing the unique challenges they face. By fostering safe spaces, providing mental health support, and promoting self-acceptance, these resources and organizations contribute to the overall well-being and empowerment of LGBTQ+ Muslim youth. International attorneys can play a vital role in advocating for the rights of LGBTQ+ Muslim youth by familiarizing themselves with these resources and organizations and using their legal expertise to support their work.

Strategies for Coming Out in a Religious and Cultural Context

Coming out as LGBTQ+ in a religious and cultural context can pose unique challenges for individuals belonging to Muslim communities.

The intersection of one's sexual orientation or gender identity with their religious beliefs and cultural norms can create a complex and often difficult journey. However, with careful consideration and support, it is possible to navigate this process while staying true to oneself and maintaining relationships with loved ones. Here are some strategies to consider:

1. Self-reflection and Education: Before coming out, take the time to understand your own identity, beliefs, and values. Educate yourself about LGBTQ+ issues within the Muslim community and explore alternative interpretations of religious texts that are inclusive and accepting.

2. Seek Support: Reach out to support networks specifically designed for LGBTQ+ Muslims. These communities can provide a safe space where you can share your experiences, gain advice, and find understanding from others who have gone through similar journeys.

3. Choose the Right Time and Place: Timing is crucial when coming out to family or friends. Consider selecting a calm and private setting where you can have an open conversation without distractions. It may also help to choose a time when your loved ones are more likely to be receptive, such as after a positive event or when they are in a relaxed state of mind.

4. Start with Allies: Identify supportive individuals within your community or family who may be more open-minded and understanding. Coming out to them first can provide a support system and potentially help in navigating conversations with others.

5. Communicate Clearly and Respectfully: Clearly express your feelings, experiences, and journey while being respectful of others' beliefs and emotions. Emphasize that your identity does not diminish your faith but is an integral part of who you are.

6. Provide Resources: Offer educational materials, books, or articles that promote understanding and acceptance of LGBTQ+ individuals within

an Islamic framework. These resources can help dispel misconceptions and provide a foundation for dialogue.

7. Patience and Resilience: Coming out can be met with a range of reactions, including resistance, confusion, or even rejection. It is important to be patient and give your loved ones time to process this information. Remember that everyone's journey is different, and it may take time for them to fully understand and accept your identity.

Navigating the intersection of homosexuality and Islam can be challenging, but it is possible to find acceptance and support within Muslim communities. By employing these strategies, individuals can come out while fostering understanding, dialogue, and positive change within their religious and cultural contexts.

Chapter 6: Support Networks for LGBTQ+ Muslims

Importance of Support Networks for LGBTQ+ Muslims

Title: Importance of Support Networks for LGBTQ+ Muslims

Introduction:

Support networks play a crucial role in the lives of LGBTQ+ Muslims, offering them a lifeline in their journey of self-acceptance, resilience, and empowerment. These networks provide a safe space for individuals navigating the complex intersections of their sexual orientation, gender identity, and their faith within Muslim communities. This subchapter explores the significance of support networks for LGBTQ+ Muslims, highlighting their vital role in fostering acceptance, resilience, and advocating for their rights.

Creating Safe Spaces:

Support networks provide LGBTQ+ Muslims with a safe and non-judgmental environment where they can freely express their identities and experiences. These inclusive spaces enable individuals to find solace, connect with like-minded peers, and share their stories without the fear of rejection or discrimination. By nurturing a sense of belonging, support networks empower LGBTQ+ Muslims to embrace their authentic selves while fostering a positive sense of community.

Emotional and Mental Well-being:

Support networks offer a vital source of emotional and mental well-being for LGBTQ+ Muslims. These networks provide access to counseling, mental health resources, and peer support groups, addressing the unique challenges faced by individuals who often grapple with conflicting identities. By offering a space to discuss personal struggles, support networks help LGBTQ+ Muslims navigate the complex emotional journey, promote self-acceptance, and build resilience.

Advocacy and Visibility:

Support networks play a pivotal role in advocating for LGBTQ+ rights within Muslim communities. By amplifying the voices and experiences of LGBTQ+ Muslims, these networks challenge societal prejudices, dismantle stereotypes, and promote inclusivity. They engage in grassroots activism, organizing events, and campaigns, raising awareness about the challenges faced by LGBTQ+ Muslims and advocating for their rights to be recognized and protected.

Intersectionality and Inclusivity:

Support networks for LGBTQ+ Muslims recognize the importance of intersectionality, acknowledging that LGBTQ+ individuals may also face other forms of marginalization based on race, ethnicity, class, or disability. These networks promote inclusivity by addressing the unique challenges faced by LGBTQ+ Muslims at the intersections of multiple identities, fostering a sense of solidarity and empowerment.

Conclusion:

Support networks are invaluable in the lives of LGBTQ+ Muslims, providing a lifeline of acceptance, resilience, and empowerment. By creating safe spaces, promoting mental well-being, advocating for rights, and acknowledging intersectionality, these networks play a crucial role in enabling LGBTQ+ Muslims to navigate their unique journeys. As international attorneys, it is vital to recognize and support the importance of such networks in promoting LGBTQ+ rights advocacy in Muslim communities, ensuring that the voices and rights of LGBTQ+ Muslims are heard and respected worldwide.

Existing Support Networks and Organizations

In recent years, there has been a growing recognition of the challenges faced by LGBTQ+ individuals in the Muslim world. As international attorneys, it is essential to understand the existing support networks and organizations that play a crucial role in advocating for LGBTQ+ rights and providing assistance to individuals facing discrimination and persecution based on their sexual orientation or gender identity.

One of the key organizations working tirelessly to support LGBTQ+ individuals in the Muslim world is the Muslim Alliance for Sexual and Gender Diversity (MASGD). MASGD serves as a platform for LGBTQ+ Muslims to connect, share experiences, and find support within their faith communities. They provide resources, organize events, and offer a safe space for LGBTQ+ Muslims to discuss intersectional issues faced within their communities.

Another notable organization is the Al-Fatiha Foundation, which focuses on providing support and resources for LGBTQ+ Muslims. Al-Fatiha has been instrumental in challenging the prevalent stigma and discrimination faced by LGBTQ+ individuals and promoting inclusive interpretations of Islam. They offer counseling services, organize conferences, and engage in advocacy work to promote acceptance and understanding within Muslim communities.

The LGBTQ+ Muslim Youth Network (LMYN) is a much-needed support network specifically catering to the unique challenges faced by LGBTQ+ Muslim youth. LMYN provides a safe space for young individuals to connect, share experiences, and find mentorship and guidance. This organization plays a vital role in empowering LGBTQ+ Muslim youth to navigate their identities within the context of their faith and culture.

Additionally, organizations such as the International Gay and Lesbian Human Rights Commission (IGLHRC) and Human Rights Watch are actively involved in advocating for LGBTQ+ rights globally, including in Muslim-majority countries. They conduct research, document human rights abuses, and engage in legal and policy advocacy to promote equality and justice for LGBTQ+ individuals.

It is worth mentioning that the visibility and representation of LGBTQ+ Muslims in media and arts have been growing, thanks to initiatives like the Queer Muslim Project and various LGBTQ+ Muslim artists. These platforms challenge stereotypes and provide a voice for LGBTQ+ Muslims, contributing to a broader understanding and acceptance of their experiences.

While progress has been made, it is crucial to recognize the ongoing challenges faced by LGBTQ+ Muslims, especially those who are refugees or asylum seekers. Organizations like the Organization for Refuge, Asylum, and Migration (ORAM) provide critical support to LGBTQ+ individuals fleeing persecution, helping them navigate the complex processes of seeking asylum and resettlement.

In conclusion, the existence of support networks and organizations dedicated to LGBTQ+ Muslims is a testament to the resilience and determination of individuals advocating for change within their communities. As international attorneys, it is our responsibility to collaborate with these organizations, support their efforts, and work towards promoting equality and justice for LGBTQ+ individuals in the Muslim world. Understanding the challenges and experiences of LGBTQ+ Muslims within the context of their faith and culture is crucial for effective advocacy and legal representation.

Creating Safe Spaces and Community Building

In the fight for LGBTQ+ rights, one of the most crucial aspects is the creation of safe spaces and the building of strong and supportive communities. This subchapter explores the various challenges faced by LGBTQ+ individuals in the Muslim world and the strategies used to overcome them, with a focus on legal challenges and advocacy efforts.

For many LGBTQ+ individuals in Muslim communities, the struggle for acceptance and understanding is a constant battle. Discrimination, violence, and social stigma can make it extremely difficult for them to express their true selves openly. This subchapter aims to provide international attorneys with a comprehensive understanding of the unique challenges faced by LGBTQ+ individuals in the Muslim world and equip them with the necessary tools to advocate for their rights effectively.

The chapter begins by exploring the legal landscape surrounding homosexuality in Muslim-majority countries. It delves into the complex intersection of religious beliefs, cultural norms, and legal frameworks that shape the lived experiences of LGBTQ+ individuals. Through case studies and legal analyses, international attorneys can gain insights into the legal challenges faced by LGBTQ+ individuals and the strategies employed to navigate these obstacles.

Furthermore, this subchapter highlights the importance of community building and support networks for LGBTQ+ Muslims. It explores the experiences of LGBTQ+ Muslims who have found solace and empowerment through organized groups and initiatives. By shedding light on these success stories, international attorneys can learn from the strategies employed in these community-building efforts and apply them to their own advocacy work.

The subchapter also addresses the critical issue of intersectionality, examining the experiences of LGBTQ+ Muslims who belong to other marginalized identities. It emphasizes the need for an inclusive and intersectional approach to advocacy, recognizing that the struggle for LGBTQ+ rights cannot be divorced from other forms of discrimination and oppression.

Finally, this subchapter explores the representation and visibility of LGBTQ+ Muslims in media, arts, and literature. It celebrates the courageous individuals who have used their creativity and platforms to challenge stereotypes and promote understanding. By amplifying their voices, international attorneys can contribute to the progress of LGBTQ+ rights in the Muslim world.

In conclusion, this subchapter on creating safe spaces and community building provides international attorneys with a comprehensive understanding of the challenges faced by LGBTQ+ individuals in the Muslim world. By equipping them with knowledge, strategies, and case studies, it empowers attorneys to effectively advocate for the rights of LGBTQ+ individuals and contribute to the ongoing struggle for equality and acceptance.

Chapter 7: Representation and Visibility of LGBTQ+ Muslims in Media and Arts

Media Representation of LGBTQ+ Muslims

Media representation plays a crucial role in shaping public perceptions and understanding of LGBTQ+ Muslims. This subchapter explores the various ways in which the media portrays and represents LGBTQ+ Muslims, examining both positive and negative aspects. It delves into the implications of media representation on the lives of LGBTQ+ Muslims, their struggles, and the challenges they face.

The media has often perpetuated stereotypes and misrepresentations of LGBTQ+ Muslims, further marginalizing and stigmatizing their experiences. Negative portrayals often focus on sensationalizing stories, emphasizing conflict between religious beliefs and sexual orientation, and promoting Islamophobia. These representations not only contribute to societal prejudice but also hinder progress towards acceptance and understanding within Muslim communities.

However, there have been positive shifts in media representation, with increasing efforts to provide more accurate and diverse portrayals of LGBTQ+ Muslims. These representations aim to challenge stereotypes, highlight the experiences and struggles of LGBTQ+ Muslims, and promote acceptance and inclusivity within their communities. By showcasing the stories and voices of LGBTQ+ Muslims, the media can help break down barriers and foster dialogue, leading to greater acceptance and support for LGBTQ+ rights advocacy in Muslim communities.

Intersectionality is another crucial aspect explored in this subchapter. It examines how LGBTQ+ Muslims navigate the intersections of their sexual orientation, gender identity, and other marginalized identities, such as race, ethnicity, and disability. The media's representation of these intersecting identities plays a significant role in shaping public understanding and empathy towards LGBTQ+ Muslims.

The subchapter also delves into the experiences of LGBTQ+ Muslim youth, discussing the challenges they face, including coming out to their families and communities. It explores the support networks available for LGBTQ+ Muslims, highlighting the importance of safe spaces and organizations that provide resources, counseling, and community support.

Furthermore, this subchapter examines the representation and visibility of LGBTQ+ Muslims in media and arts, discussing the impact of positive representation on dismantling stereotypes and fostering acceptance. It also explores LGBTQ+ Muslim activism, organizing, and the role of queer theology in interpreting Islam.

Lastly, this subchapter addresses the unique experiences and challenges faced by LGBTQ+ Muslim refugees and asylum seekers. It explores their struggles in finding acceptance and support in new countries and the importance of creating inclusive environments for LGBTQ+ Muslim diaspora communities.

Overall, this subchapter aims to provide international attorneys with a comprehensive understanding of media representation of LGBTQ+ Muslims. It highlights the importance of accurate and diverse portrayals, challenges prevailing stereotypes, and emphasizes the need for greater acceptance, support, and inclusion within Muslim communities.

Impact of LGBTQ+ Muslim Representation on Society

Introduction:

The representation of LGBTQ+ Muslims in society has been a topic of great significance and debate. In recent years, there has been a growing recognition of the importance of LGBTQ+ Muslim representation in media, arts, and advocacy work. This subchapter explores the impact of LGBTQ+ Muslim representation on society, focusing on the legal challenges and advocacy efforts of international attorneys.

Legal Challenges and Advocacy:

International attorneys play a crucial role in addressing the legal challenges faced by LGBTQ+ Muslims in the Muslim world. They work towards advocating for equal rights, combating discrimination, and challenging oppressive laws that criminalize homosexuality. By shedding light on these issues and engaging in legal battles, international attorneys help shape public opinion and contribute to the changing legal landscape.

Intersectionality and Marginalized Identities:

The experiences of LGBTQ+ Muslims intersect with various marginalized identities, such as race, ethnicity, gender, and socioeconomic status. International attorneys must understand these intersections to effectively advocate for the rights of LGBTQ+ Muslims. By recognizing the unique challenges faced by individuals with multiple marginalized identities, they can work towards a more inclusive and equitable society.

Representation in Media and Arts:

The representation and visibility of LGBTQ+ Muslims in media and arts play a crucial role in challenging stereotypes and promoting understanding. International attorneys can collaborate with artists, filmmakers, and writers to ensure accurate and positive portrayals of LGBTQ+ Muslims. This representation helps challenge societal prejudices, foster empathy, and contribute to the broader acceptance of LGBTQ+ Muslims in society.

Support Networks and Activism:

International attorneys can also support LGBTQ+ Muslim individuals by assisting in the establishment of support networks and advocacy organizations. These networks provide a safe space for LGBTQ+ Muslims to connect, share experiences, and seek support. LGBTQ+ Muslim activism and organizing are essential for creating change and challenging harmful narratives.

Queer Theology and Interpretations of Islam:

The intersection of LGBTQ+ identities and religious beliefs is a complex and often challenging issue. International attorneys can engage with scholars, theologians, and community leaders to promote interpretations of Islam that are inclusive and affirming of LGBTQ+ individuals. By encouraging the development of queer theology and alternative interpretations, international attorneys contribute to a more accepting and inclusive religious landscape.

Conclusion:

The impact of LGBTQ+ Muslim representation on society is significant and multifaceted. International attorneys play a crucial role in challenging legal barriers, advocating for LGBTQ+ Muslim rights, and fostering understanding and acceptance. By addressing legal challenges, promoting representation in media and arts, supporting networks and activism, and encouraging inclusive interpretations of Islam, international attorneys contribute to a more equitable and accepting society for LGBTQ+ Muslims worldwide.

Promoting Positive and Diverse Representations

In a world where diversity and inclusivity are increasingly valued, it is crucial to promote positive and diverse representations of LGBTQ+ individuals, particularly in the Muslim world. This subchapter explores the importance of representation and visibility, and how it can contribute to the advancement of LGBTQ+ rights advocacy in Muslim communities.

Representation matters. When LGBTQ+ individuals see positive and diverse portrayals of themselves in media, arts, and literature, it not only validates their identities but also helps combat the stigma and discrimination they face. By showcasing the stories, struggles, and achievements of LGBTQ+ Muslims, we can challenge stereotypes and foster understanding within Muslim communities.

Media and arts play a vital role in shaping public perceptions. Therefore, it is essential to encourage the production and dissemination of content that reflects the diversity of LGBTQ+ Muslims. This can be done through films, documentaries, books, and art exhibitions that explore the intersectionality of LGBTQ+ identities and other marginalized identities within Muslim communities. By highlighting the experiences of LGBTQ+ Muslims, we can amplify their voices and create empathy among international audiences.

Furthermore, promoting positive representations goes beyond media and arts. It extends to the realm of activism, organizing, and legal advocacy. LGBTQ+ Muslim activists and organizations play a crucial role in challenging discriminatory laws and policies, advocating for equal rights, and creating safe spaces for LGBTQ+ Muslims. By elevating their work and achievements, we can inspire and empower others to join the fight for LGBTQ+ rights in Muslim communities.

Visibility is not only about representation but also about acknowledging and supporting the unique challenges faced by LGBTQ+ Muslims. This includes addressing the experiences of LGBTQ+ Muslim youth, their struggles with coming out, and the need for support networks within their communities. It also encompasses the experiences of LGBTQ+

Muslim refugees and asylum seekers, as well as the diaspora communities they form in new countries.

In conclusion, promoting positive and diverse representations of LGBTQ+ Muslims is crucial for advancing LGBTQ+ rights advocacy in the Muslim world. By highlighting their stories, challenging stereotypes, and fostering understanding, we can contribute to the creation of more inclusive and accepting societies. This subchapter explores the intersectionality of LGBTQ+ identities within Muslim communities and provides insights into the challenges, experiences, and achievements of LGBTQ+ Muslims. Through increased visibility and representation, we can pave the way for a future where LGBTQ+ individuals in the Muslim world can live authentically and without fear of discrimination.

Chapter 8: LGBTQ+ Muslim Activism and Organizing

History and Evolution of LGBTQ+ Muslim Activism

Introduction:

The history and evolution of LGBTQ+ Muslim activism is a complex and multifaceted journey that has spanned several decades. This subchapter explores the significant milestones, challenges, and triumphs experienced by LGBTQ+ activists within Muslim communities. By examining the historical context, we can better understand the current state of LGBTQ+ rights advocacy in the Muslim world.

The Emergence of LGBTQ+ Muslim Activism:

LGBTQ+ Muslim activism began to gain traction in the late 20th century, as marginalized voices within Muslim communities sought to challenge the prevailing narratives that excluded or oppressed sexual and gender minorities. Activists started organizing in various countries, often facing legal, social, and religious barriers.

Early Challenges and Experiences:

During this period, LGBTQ+ Muslims faced significant challenges, including the criminalization of homosexuality, societal stigma, and the clash between religious teachings and sexual orientations. Activists worked tirelessly to raise awareness, challenge discriminatory laws, and promote acceptance within their communities.

Intersectionality and Marginalized Identities:

Recognizing the intersectionality of LGBTQ+ Muslims, activists started addressing the multiple layers of discrimination faced by individuals who belonged to other marginalized groups, such as women, people of color, and disabled individuals. This inclusive approach helped to create a more comprehensive understanding of the struggles faced by LGBTQ+ Muslims.

Support Networks and Coming Out:

Support networks, both online and offline, emerged as safe spaces for LGBTQ+ Muslims to share their experiences, seek guidance, and find solace. Coming out stories became an essential tool for increasing visibility, challenging stereotypes, and fostering acceptance within Muslim communities.

Representation and Visibility:

The representation of LGBTQ+ Muslims in media and the arts played a vital role in challenging stereotypes and facilitating dialogue. Books, movies, and art projects highlighted the experiences and perspectives of LGBTQ+ Muslims, contributing to a more inclusive narrative.

Organizing and Activism:

LGBTQ+ Muslim activists organized conferences, seminars, and workshops to create a platform for dialogue and advocacy. The establishment of LGBTQ+ Muslim organizations and alliances further strengthened the movement, enabling activists to collaborate and amplify their voices.

Queer Theology and Interpretations of Islam:

A significant development within LGBTQ+ Muslim activism was the emergence of queer theology, which reinterpreted Islamic teachings to be inclusive of sexual and gender diversity. These alternative interpretations provided LGBTQ+ Muslims with a theological basis for their existence and rights within Islam.

Refugees, Asylum Seekers, and Diaspora Communities:

The plight of LGBTQ+ Muslim refugees and asylum seekers highlighted the need for international legal protections and support networks. Diaspora communities played a crucial role in providing a sense of belonging, support, and advocacy for LGBTQ+ Muslims who faced persecution in their home countries.

Conclusion:

The history and evolution of LGBTQ+ Muslim activism is a testament to the resilience, determination, and perseverance of individuals fighting for their rights within Muslim communities. The journey has been marked by progress, setbacks, and ongoing challenges. However, the increasing visibility, support networks, and inclusive interpretations of Islam provide hope for a more inclusive future where LGBTQ+ Muslims can freely express their identities and live without fear of discrimination. International attorneys have a crucial role to play in advocating for legal protections and supporting the rights of LGBTQ+ Muslims in the Muslim world and beyond.

Strategies and Tactics for LGBTQ+ Muslim Activism

In the fight for LGBTQ+ rights and inclusion within Muslim communities, activists face unique challenges that require strategic approaches and thoughtful tactics. This subchapter explores effective strategies and tactics for LGBTQ+ Muslim activism, providing guidance for international attorneys working in this field.

1. Building Alliances: LGBTQ+ Muslim activists should actively seek alliances with other marginalized groups, recognizing the importance of intersectionality. Collaborating with organizations advocating for women's rights, racial equality, and religious freedom can help amplify their voices and push for broader societal change.

2. Grassroots Organizing: Creating safe spaces for LGBTQ+ Muslims to meet, share experiences, and organize is crucial. Building local support networks and organizing community events, such as workshops, conferences, and awareness campaigns, can foster dialogue and understanding within Muslim communities.

3. Legal Advocacy: International attorneys can play a vital role in supporting LGBTQ+ Muslim activists by providing legal expertise and guidance. This includes challenging discriminatory laws and policies, advocating for legal protections, and offering pro bono services to LGBTQ+ Muslims facing legal challenges.

4. Media and Arts Representation: Encouraging positive representation of LGBTQ+ Muslims in media and the arts is essential for challenging stereotypes and shifting societal attitudes. Activists can collaborate with filmmakers, writers, and artists to create authentic and diverse narratives that showcase the experiences of LGBTQ+ Muslims.

5. Engaging Religious Leaders: Engaging with progressive religious leaders can help challenge homophobic interpretations of Islamic teachings. By highlighting inclusive interpretations and promoting queer theology, activists can foster a more accepting environment within Muslim communities.

6. Supporting LGBTQ+ Muslim Youth: LGBTQ+ Muslim youth often face unique challenges, including coming out to their families and communities. Providing support networks, counseling services, and mentorship programs can help empower and guide these young individuals.

7. Advocacy for Refugees and Asylum Seekers: LGBTQ+ Muslims fleeing persecution in their home countries often face additional challenges when seeking asylum. Advocacy efforts should focus on

raising awareness about their specific needs and ensuring their protection and inclusion in host countries.

8. Empowering Diaspora Communities: LGBTQ+ Muslim activists should work towards creating safe spaces and support networks within diaspora communities. Celebrating diverse identities and experiences can help combat isolation and promote a sense of belonging.

By employing these strategies and tactics, international attorneys can play a crucial role in supporting LGBTQ+ Muslim activism. This subchapter aims to equip them with the necessary knowledge and tools to navigate the complex challenges faced by LGBTQ+ Muslims in the Muslim world, promoting equality, inclusion, and justice for all.

Collaborations and Alliances with Other Movements

In the fight for LGBTQ+ rights in the Muslim world, collaborations and alliances with other movements are essential for creating meaningful change. Recognizing the power of collective action, many LGBTQ+ advocacy groups have sought partnerships with diverse organizations and movements, aiming to amplify their voices and leverage their impact.

One crucial aspect of collaboration is the intersectionality between LGBTQ+ Muslims and other marginalized identities. By joining forces with social justice movements addressing racism, gender inequality, and religious discrimination, LGBTQ+ Muslims can forge strong alliances that challenge systemic oppression holistically. These collaborations can help create safe spaces for LGBTQ+ Muslims to express their intersecting identities and provide a platform for their unique experiences to be acknowledged.

Furthermore, collaborations can also foster support networks for LGBTQ+ Muslims. By working with mental health organizations, community centers, and religious institutions, LGBTQ+ Muslims can establish inclusive spaces where individuals can find solace, connect with others facing similar challenges, and access the resources they need. These partnerships can help create a sense of belonging and reduce the isolation often experienced by LGBTQ+ Muslims, particularly youth who may be struggling with their sexual orientation or gender identity.

Collaborations and alliances are also crucial for advocating for LGBTQ+ Muslim refugees and asylum seekers. By partnering with human rights organizations, legal aid groups, and refugee support networks, LGBTQ+ activists can amplify the voices of those fleeing persecution and work towards creating inclusive policies and practices that protect their rights. These collaborations can provide much-needed support to individuals navigating the complex legal systems and aid in securing safe spaces for LGBTQ+ Muslim refugees and asylum seekers.

In addition to advocacy, collaborations with media and arts organizations can help increase the representation and visibility of LGBTQ+ Muslims. By working together, activists and artists can challenge stereotypes, break down barriers, and offer alternative narratives that celebrate the diversity within LGBTQ+ Muslim communities. This collaboration can pave the way for greater acceptance and understanding, fostering an environment where LGBTQ+ Muslims feel seen and validated.

Overall, collaborations and alliances between LGBTQ+ rights movements and various organizations addressing social justice issues are crucial for navigating homosexualism in the Muslim world. By leveraging the collective power of diverse groups, international attorneys, and advocates can work towards dismantling systemic oppression and creating a more inclusive and accepting society for LGBTQ+ Muslims worldwide.

Chapter 9: Queer Theology and Interpretations of Islam

Exploration of Queer Theology within Islamic Context

Within the complex landscape of LGBTQ+ rights advocacy in Muslim communities, one area that is gaining attention is the exploration of queer theology within an Islamic context. This subchapter aims to delve into this emerging field, highlighting the challenges and experiences faced by LGBTQ+ Muslims, the intersectionality of their identities, and the potential for activism and organizing within this unique framework.

Queer theology, at its core, seeks to reconcile religious beliefs and LGBTQ+ identities. It challenges traditional interpretations of religious texts and doctrines, seeking to create space for the inclusion and acceptance of diverse sexual orientations and gender identities within religious communities. In an Islamic context, this exploration becomes particularly significant, as it engages with the teachings of the Quran and the Hadith to create a more inclusive understanding of Islam.

While queer theology within an Islamic context is still in its nascent stages, there have been notable efforts to reinterpret Islamic texts and traditions in a way that affirms and supports LGBTQ+ Muslims. Scholars and theologians are engaging in rigorous research and dialogue to develop alternative interpretations that challenge the prevailing heteronormative and cisnormative narratives within the Muslim world.

However, navigating queer theology within an Islamic context is not without its challenges. LGBTQ+ Muslims often face opposition from conservative religious leaders and communities who view homosexuality as incompatible with Islam. This subchapter will explore the legal challenges faced by LGBTQ+ Muslims, including the criminalization of homosexuality in some Muslim-majority countries, and the implications for advocacy efforts.

Additionally, the subchapter will address the experiences of LGBTQ+ Muslim youth, who often struggle with issues of coming out, acceptance, and the intersectionality of their multiple identities. It will also highlight the importance of support networks for LGBTQ+ Muslims, both within and outside of religious spaces.

Furthermore, the subchapter will shed light on the representation and visibility of LGBTQ+ Muslims in media and arts. It will explore the role of storytelling and artistic expression in challenging stereotypes and fostering understanding and empathy.

Lastly, the subchapter will examine the experiences of LGBTQ+ Muslim refugees and asylum seekers, as well as the unique challenges faced by LGBTQ+ Muslim diaspora communities. It will highlight the need for culturally competent support services and advocacy efforts tailored to their specific needs.

Overall, this subchapter aims to provide international attorneys with a comprehensive understanding of queer theology within an Islamic context. By exploring the challenges, experiences, and potential for activism within this framework, it seeks to foster dialogue and engagement among legal professionals working in the fields of LGBTQ+ rights advocacy and Muslim communities.

Alternative Interpretations of Islamic Texts

In the quest for LGBTQ+ rights advocacy in the Muslim world, one of the key challenges faced by international attorneys is navigating the interpretation of Islamic texts. Islamic texts, such as the Quran and Hadiths, have often been used to justify the marginalization and persecution of LGBTQ+ individuals. However, there exists a growing movement within Muslim communities that offers alternative interpretations of these texts, providing a more inclusive and accepting view of homosexuality.

These alternative interpretations emphasize the principles of compassion, justice, and equality that are central to Islam. They argue that the condemnation of homosexuality in traditional interpretations is based on cultural biases and misinterpretations rather than the true teachings of Islam. Scholars and activists promoting these alternative interpretations argue that Islam, as a religion, should evolve and adapt to the changing social and cultural contexts of the modern world.

One such alternative interpretation focuses on re-examining key Quranic verses that are often used to condemn homosexuality. Advocates argue that these verses should be read in their historical and cultural context, taking into account the prevailing attitudes towards same-sex relationships at the time. They point out that the Quran does not explicitly condemn same-sex relationships but rather focuses on the importance of consent, respect, and avoiding harm in all relationships.

Another alternative interpretation looks at the concept of "ijtihad," which encourages independent reasoning and interpretation in Islamic jurisprudence. Proponents argue that this principle allows for a more nuanced understanding of homosexuality, recognizing that societal attitudes and scientific knowledge have evolved since the time these texts were written. They believe that Islamic law should reflect the realities and needs of contemporary society, including the recognition and protection of LGBTQ+ rights.

These alternative interpretations provide a foundation for legal challenges and advocacy for LGBTQ+ rights in the Muslim world. By engaging with Islamic texts in a critical and progressive manner, international attorneys can challenge the dominant narrative and promote a more inclusive understanding of Islam. This approach is crucial in countering the legal and cultural barriers faced by LGBTQ+ individuals in Muslim communities.

By highlighting these alternative interpretations, this subchapter aims to inform and empower international attorneys working in the niches of homosexualism in the Muslim world, LGBTQ+ rights advocacy in Muslim communities, and the challenges and experiences of LGBTQ+ Muslims. It explores the intersectionality of LGBTQ+ Muslims with other marginalized identities and emphasizes the importance of support networks, representation, and visibility in media and arts. The subchapter also delves into the role of queer theology in shaping interpretations of Islam, the unique challenges faced by LGBTQ+ Muslim refugees and asylum seekers, and the experiences of LGBTQ+ Muslim diaspora communities. Ultimately, it seeks to foster dialogue and understanding between different stakeholders and contribute to the advancement of LGBTQ+ rights in the Muslim world.

Reconciling Faith and Sexual Orientation

One of the most complex and challenging aspects faced by LGBTQ+ individuals in the Muslim world is reconciling their faith with their sexual orientation. This subchapter aims to explore the various perspectives, challenges, and experiences that arise when attempting to navigate the intersection of faith and sexual orientation.

For many LGBTQ+ individuals in Muslim communities, there is a deep sense of conflict between their religious beliefs and their sexual orientation. Traditional interpretations of Islam often view homosexuality as sinful or forbidden, leading to feelings of guilt, shame, and isolation. This subchapter seeks to address these concerns and provide guidance to international attorneys working with LGBTQ+ individuals in the Muslim world.

Navigating the complexities of faith and sexual orientation requires a delicate balance between religious teachings and personal identity. It is essential to foster an inclusive and respectful dialogue that acknowledges the diversity of interpretations within Islam and promotes acceptance and understanding. International attorneys can play a pivotal role in advocating for LGBTQ+ rights within Muslim communities, highlighting the importance of legal challenges and the need for change.

Furthermore, this subchapter explores the experiences of LGBTQ+ Muslims, shedding light on the unique challenges they face due to their intersecting identities. It delves into the concept of intersectionality and examines how LGBTQ+ Muslims navigate their sexual orientation alongside other marginalized identities such as race, gender, and socioeconomic status.

Additionally, this subchapter addresses the experiences of LGBTQ+ Muslim youth, their struggles with coming out, and the support networks available to them. It emphasizes the importance of creating safe spaces and fostering understanding within families, schools, and communities.

Representation and visibility of LGBTQ+ Muslims in media and arts is another crucial aspect discussed within this subchapter. By showcasing diverse narratives and challenging stereotypes, LGBTQ+ Muslims can find solace and inspiration, while also challenging societal norms and prejudices.

Lastly, this chapter explores the activism and organizing efforts of LGBTQ+ Muslims, providing guidance and resources for attorneys working with these communities. It also delves into the emerging field of queer theology and interpretations of Islam, offering alternative perspectives that reconcile faith and sexual orientation.

Ultimately, this subchapter aims to empower international attorneys to effectively navigate the complex issues surrounding faith and sexual orientation in the Muslim world. By understanding the challenges faced by LGBTQ+ individuals, promoting inclusivity, and advocating for legal change, attorneys can play a significant role in advancing LGBTQ+ rights within Muslim communities worldwide.

Chapter 10: LGBTQ+ Muslim Refugees and Asylum Seekers

Challenges Faced by LGBTQ+ Muslim Refugees and Asylum Seekers

In recent years, the plight of LGBTQ+ individuals seeking refuge and asylum has garnered significant attention worldwide. However, the challenges faced by LGBTQ+ Muslim refugees and asylum seekers are particularly complex due to the intersectionality of their identities and the cultural and religious barriers they encounter. This subchapter aims to shed light on the unique struggles faced by this marginalized community and offers insights for international attorneys working in this field.

One of the most significant challenges faced by LGBTQ+ Muslim refugees and asylum seekers is the fear of persecution from their own communities. In many Muslim-majority countries, homosexuality is criminalized, and individuals can face severe penalties, including imprisonment and even death. Fleeing their home countries, these individuals often find themselves isolated and vulnerable, grappling with cultural and religious conflicts that compound their already precarious situation.

Additionally, LGBTQ+ Muslim refugees and asylum seekers often face discrimination and prejudice within the host countries they seek refuge in. These individuals may encounter hostility from fellow refugees, as well as from the wider society, due to the intersectionality of their LGBTQ+ and Muslim identities. This can lead to social exclusion, limited access to housing, employment, and healthcare, and even violence.

The lack of support networks and resources specifically tailored to the needs of LGBTQ+ Muslim refugees and asylum seekers further exacerbates their challenges. Many existing support services are not equipped to address the unique needs and experiences of this community, leaving them feeling marginalized and without access to vital assistance.

Another crucial issue is the limited visibility and representation of LGBTQ+ Muslim individuals in media, arts, and public narratives. This lack of representation perpetuates stereotypes and reinforces the notion that being both LGBTQ+ and Muslim is incompatible. International attorneys can play a vital role in advocating for increased visibility and representation, challenging societal biases, and fostering a more inclusive and accepting environment for LGBTQ+ Muslim refugees and asylum seekers.

Furthermore, legal challenges related to the asylum process itself pose significant barriers for LGBTQ+ Muslim individuals. The burden of proof to establish their sexual orientation or gender identity can be particularly challenging, especially in cases where the individual may not have openly identified as LGBTQ+ prior to seeking asylum. International attorneys can provide crucial support in navigating these legal challenges, ensuring that LGBTQ+ Muslims are not wrongly denied asylum based on cultural misunderstandings or biases.

In conclusion, the challenges faced by LGBTQ+ Muslim refugees and asylum seekers are multi-faceted and require a comprehensive and intersectional approach. International attorneys have a pivotal role to play in advocating for the rights and protection of this marginalized community, working towards the creation of inclusive policies, and fostering greater awareness and understanding within both Muslim communities and broader society.

Legal Protections and Policies for LGBTQ+ Muslim Refugees

Introduction:

As the global conversation around LGBTQ+ rights continues to evolve, it is crucial to address the unique challenges faced by LGBTQ+ Muslim refugees. This subchapter explores the legal protections and policies that can support and advocate for this marginalized community, ensuring their safety and well-being within host countries. By understanding the intersectionality of their identities, the international legal community can play a vital role in creating inclusive environments for LGBTQ+ Muslim refugees.

Legal Challenges and Advocacy:

LGBTQ+ Muslims seeking refuge often face immense legal challenges. Many countries lack comprehensive protections for LGBTQ+ individuals, and this is compounded by cultural and religious barriers within Muslim communities. International attorneys must advocate for legal frameworks that recognize the specific vulnerabilities and needs of LGBTQ+ Muslim refugees, ensuring their access to asylum and protection from persecution.

National and International Policies:

Efficient policies are necessary to address the complexities of LGBTQ+ Muslim refugees' experiences. International attorneys can work towards the adoption and implementation of policies that promote the rights of sexual and gender minorities within the context of Islam. This includes recognizing sexual orientation and gender identity as grounds for asylum, providing comprehensive healthcare, and protecting LGBTQ+ individuals from discrimination and violence.

Intersectionality and Marginalized Identities:

LGBTQ+ Muslim refugees often experience multiple forms of marginalization, including racism, xenophobia, and Islamophobia. International attorneys must recognize and address the intersectionality of their clients' identities, advocating for policies that protect them from overlapping forms of discrimination. This requires collaboration with other advocacy groups focused on racial and religious minorities to create inclusive spaces for LGBTQ+ Muslims.

Support Networks and Visibility:

Creating support networks for LGBTQ+ Muslim refugees is crucial for their well-being and mental health. International attorneys can play a vital role in fostering these networks by collaborating with NGOs, community organizations, and religious leaders who are open to supporting LGBTQ+ individuals. Additionally, promoting positive representation and visibility of LGBTQ+ Muslims in media and arts can challenge stereotypes and misconceptions, ultimately contributing to a more accepting society.

Conclusion:

International attorneys play a critical role in advocating for legal protections and policies that address the unique challenges faced by LGBTQ+ Muslim refugees. By recognizing the intersectionality of their identities, collaborating with advocacy groups, and fostering support networks, attorneys can help create inclusive environments where LGBTQ+ Muslim refugees can thrive. It is through these efforts that we can navigate the complexities of homosexualism in the Muslim world and ensure the rights and well-being of all individuals, irrespective of their sexual orientation, gender identity, or religious beliefs.

Support Services and Resources for LGBTQ+ Muslim Refugees

Introduction:

The intersectionality of being both LGBTQ+ and Muslim presents unique challenges for individuals seeking refuge due to persecution based on their sexual orientation or gender identity. This subchapter focuses on the support services and resources available to LGBTQ+

Muslim refugees, aiming to provide international attorneys with a comprehensive understanding of the specific needs and challenges faced by this marginalized community.

1. Legal Protections and Advocacy:

LGBTQ+ Muslim refugees require legal assistance to navigate the complex asylum process. International attorneys can play a crucial role by advocating for their rights and ensuring they receive fair treatment. This section explores existing legal protections, challenges in the asylum process, and strategies for effective representation.

2. Mental Health and Counseling:

The journey of LGBTQ+ Muslim refugees often involves traumatic experiences, including persecution, discrimination, and displacement. To address their mental health needs, support networks should include counseling services that are culturally sensitive and LGBTQ+ affirming. This section discusses the importance of mental health support and the challenges faced in providing appropriate services.

3. Social Support Networks:

Building strong social support networks is crucial for LGBTQ+ Muslim refugees, as they often face isolation and rejection from both their religious and LGBTQ+ communities. This section explores the importance of creating safe spaces, fostering peer support, and facilitating connections with other LGBTQ+ Muslim individuals and organizations.

4. Community Organizations and NGOs:

Numerous community organizations and NGOs are dedicated to supporting LGBTQ+ Muslim refugees. This section highlights the work of these organizations, their services, and the impact they have on the lives of LGBTQ+ Muslim refugees. It also emphasizes the need for collaboration between international attorneys and these organizations to provide comprehensive support.

5. Education and Empowerment:

Empowering LGBTQ+ Muslim refugees through education is crucial for their successful integration into new societies. This section discusses the importance of providing resources on LGBTQ+ rights, Islamic theology, and cultural sensitivity training for individuals and organizations working with this community.

Conclusion:

Supporting LGBTQ+ Muslim refugees requires a multifaceted approach that addresses their legal, mental health, social, and educational needs. By understanding the challenges and resources available, international attorneys can play a vital role in advocating for the rights of this marginalized group and ensuring they receive the support they need to rebuild their lives.

Chapter 11: LGBTQ+ Muslim Diaspora Communities and Experiences

Formation and Evolution of LGBTQ+ Muslim Diaspora Communities

Introduction:

The formation and evolution of LGBTQ+ Muslim diaspora communities is a complex and multifaceted phenomenon that requires a deep understanding of the intersectionality between sexual orientation, gender identity, religion, and culture. This subchapter aims to explore the challenges, experiences, and achievements of LGBTQ+ Muslims who have migrated from their home countries and established diaspora communities in various parts of the world.

1. Historical Context:

To understand the formation of LGBTQ+ Muslim diaspora communities, it is crucial to examine the historical context that has shaped their existence. This section will provide an overview of the legal, social, and cultural challenges faced by LGBTQ+ Muslims in their home countries, leading to their migration and subsequent formation of diaspora communities.

2. Diaspora Experiences:

LGBTQ+ Muslim individuals who have migrated often face unique challenges related to their sexual orientation, gender identity, and religious beliefs. This section will delve into the experiences of LGBTQ+ Muslim diaspora communities, including the struggles they face in reconciling their multiple identities, navigating cultural and religious expectations, and finding acceptance within their new societies.

3. Intersectionality and Marginalization:

The intersectionality of LGBTQ+ Muslims and other marginalized identities, such as race, ethnicity, and class, significantly impacts their experiences within diaspora communities. This section will discuss the ways in which LGBTQ+ Muslims navigate multiple layers of discrimination and marginalization, and how their experiences differ based on various intersecting identities.

4. Support Networks and Community Building:

Support networks play a vital role in the lives of LGBTQ+ Muslim diaspora communities. This section will explore the various support networks, both online and offline, that have emerged to provide a safe space and resources for LGBTQ+ Muslims, including community organizations, advocacy groups, and social media platforms.

5. Representation and Visibility:

Representation and visibility of LGBTQ+ Muslims in media and arts are crucial for challenging stereotypes and promoting acceptance. This section will examine the efforts made by LGBTQ+ Muslim activists, artists, and filmmakers to increase representation and visibility, as well as the challenges they face in doing so.

6. Activism and Organizing:

LGBTQ+ Muslim activists and organizations play a pivotal role in advocating for the rights and well-being of LGBTQ+ Muslims within diaspora communities. This section will explore the various forms of activism and organizing undertaken by LGBTQ+ Muslim individuals and groups, including advocacy campaigns, community events, and educational initiatives.

7. Queer Theology and Interpretations of Islam:

This section will discuss the emerging field of queer theology and interpretations of Islam, which seek to reconcile LGBTQ+ identities with Islamic teachings. It will explore the work of LGBTQ+ Muslim scholars, theologians, and activists who are challenging traditional interpretations and promoting inclusive understandings of Islam.

8. Refugees and Asylum Seekers:

LGBTQ+ Muslims who flee their home countries as refugees or asylum seekers face additional challenges related to their sexual orientation, gender identity, and religious beliefs. This section will explore the experiences of LGBTQ+ Muslim refugees and asylum seekers, including the barriers they face in accessing protection, support, and legal rights.

Conclusion:

The formation and evolution of LGBTQ+ Muslim diaspora communities offer a unique perspective on the intersection of sexual orientation, gender identity, and religion. By understanding the challenges, experiences, and achievements of LGBTQ+ Muslims in diaspora, international attorneys can better advocate for their rights and contribute to the broader discourse on LGBTQ+ rights advocacy in Muslim communities.

Challenges and Opportunities for LGBTQ+ Muslims in Diaspora

Introduction:

The diaspora experience for LGBTQ+ Muslims is a complex and multifaceted journey, marked by both challenges and opportunities. As international attorneys, it is crucial to understand the unique struggles faced by this community and advocate for their rights in a sensitive and informed manner. This subchapter delves into the issues surrounding Homosexualism in the Muslim World, LGBTQ+ rights advocacy in Muslim communities, challenges and experiences of LGBTQ+ Muslims, intersectionality, LGBTQ+ Muslim youth, support networks, representation and visibility, activism, queer theology, and the experiences of LGBTQ+ Muslim refugees and asylum seekers.

Homosexualism in the Muslim World:

The Muslim world is diverse and varied, encompassing a wide range of attitudes towards homosexuality. Homosexualism remains largely stigmatized and condemned in many Muslim-majority countries due to societal and religious factors. This chapter explores the legal challenges faced by LGBTQ+ Muslims in these contexts and the efforts to advocate for change.

LGBTQ+ Rights Advocacy in Muslim Communities:

Advocacy for LGBTQ+ rights in Muslim communities requires a delicate balance between respecting religious beliefs and promoting inclusivity. This subchapter examines the strategies employed by activists and organizations to challenge discriminatory practices and foster greater acceptance within Muslim communities worldwide.

Challenges and Experiences of LGBTQ+ Muslims:

LGBTQ+ Muslims face numerous challenges, including social ostracism, familial rejection, and limited access to healthcare and support services. This section explores these issues and highlights the resilience and strength demonstrated by LGBTQ+ Muslims in navigating their identities.

Intersectionality: LGBTQ+ Muslims and other marginalized identities:

The intersectionality of LGBTQ+ Muslims with other marginalized identities, such as race, gender, and disability, further complicates their experiences. This subchapter explores the unique challenges faced by

LGBTQ+ Muslims who belong to multiple marginalized communities and the need for an inclusive and intersectional approach to advocacy.

LGBTQ+ Muslim Youth and Coming Out:

Coming out as LGBTQ+ can be an especially difficult process for Muslim youth, who often grapple with conflicting cultural and religious expectations. This section discusses the challenges faced by LGBTQ+ Muslim youth and the importance of creating safe spaces and support networks for them.

Support Networks for LGBTQ+ Muslims:

Creating support networks and safe spaces is crucial for LGBTQ+ Muslims, particularly in diaspora communities. This subchapter explores the role of community organizations, online platforms, and grassroots initiatives in providing support, advocacy, and resources for LGBTQ+ Muslims.

Representation and Visibility of LGBTQ+ Muslims in Media and Arts:

The representation and visibility of LGBTQ+ Muslims in media and arts play a vital role in challenging stereotypes and fostering acceptance. This section examines the importance of diverse and authentic portrayals of LGBTQ+ Muslims and the ways in which art and media can contribute to social change.

LGBTQ+ Muslim Activism and Organizing:

LGBTQ+ Muslim activists and organizations play a pivotal role in advocating for the rights and well-being of this community. This subchapter explores the history, strategies, and achievements of LGBTQ+ Muslim activism and the challenges they face in their work.

Queer Theology and Interpretations of Islam:

This section delves into the emerging field of queer theology and its intersections with Islam. It explores the reinterpretation of Islamic texts and traditions to foster inclusivity and acceptance of LGBTQ+ Muslims within religious spaces.

LGBTQ+ Muslim Refugees and Asylum Seekers:

LGBTQ+ Muslims who seek refuge in foreign countries face unique challenges, including cultural dislocation, language barriers, and the need for legal protection. This subchapter examines the experiences of LGBTQ+ Muslim refugees and asylum seekers and the challenges they encounter in their search for safety.

LGBTQ+ Muslim Diaspora Communities and Experiences:

The diaspora experience for LGBTQ+ Muslims is shaped by a multitude of factors, including cultural preservation, integration, and identity formation. This section explores the experiences and challenges faced by LGBTQ+ Muslims in diaspora communities and highlights the importance of fostering inclusive and supportive environments.

Conclusion:

Understanding the challenges and opportunities for LGBTQ+ Muslims in diaspora is essential for international attorneys engaged in advocating for their rights. By addressing the topics of Homosexualism in the Muslim World, LGBTQ+ rights advocacy, challenges and experiences, intersectionality, support networks, representation, activism, queer theology, refugees, and diaspora communities, this subchapter aims to contribute to a more inclusive and informed dialogue surrounding LGBTQ+ Muslims. It is through this understanding that we can work towards fostering acceptance, equality, and justice for all.

Cultural Preservation and Integration in Diaspora Communities

Subchapter: Cultural Preservation and Integration in Diaspora Communities

In the ever-evolving landscape of global migration, diaspora communities play a crucial role in preserving cultural heritage while navigating the challenges of integration. This subchapter delves into the intricate balance between cultural preservation and integration within LGBTQ+ Muslim diaspora communities. By exploring the experiences, challenges, and strategies employed by these communities, this section aims to shed light on the intersectionality and unique dynamics at play.

Cultural preservation is a vital aspect of maintaining identity and fostering a sense of belonging within diaspora communities. LGBTQ+ Muslims in the diaspora often face the task of reconciling their sexual orientation or gender identity with their religious and cultural heritage. Recognizing the diversity within each diaspora community, it becomes essential to address the intersectionality of identities and explore how LGBTQ+ Muslims navigate their cultural and religious traditions while embracing their authentic selves.

Integration, on the other hand, presents a set of challenges as LGBTQ+ Muslims strive to find acceptance and inclusion within the societies they migrate to. This section will explore the legal, social, and cultural barriers faced by LGBTQ+ Muslims in diaspora communities, shedding light on the unique experiences and the strategies employed to overcome them.

The subchapter will also delve into the role of support networks and organizations that provide a safe space for LGBTQ+ Muslims to connect, share experiences, and find solidarity. These networks play a vital role in addressing the challenges faced by LGBTQ+ Muslims in the diaspora, providing resources, advocacy, and counseling services.

Furthermore, this section will examine the representation and visibility of LGBTQ+ Muslims in media and the arts, highlighting the importance of diverse narratives in shaping public perception and understanding. By amplifying voices within the LGBTQ+ Muslim community, this subchapter aims to challenge stereotypes, foster empathy, and create a more inclusive society.

Finally, the subchapter will explore the ways in which LGBTQ+ Muslims in diaspora engage in activism and organize to advocate for their rights and challenge discriminatory practices. From grassroots movements to international advocacy, LGBTQ+ Muslim activism is an essential force in driving social change and ensuring the protection of human rights.

By addressing the complex dynamics of cultural preservation and integration within LGBTQ+ Muslim diaspora communities, this subchapter provides a comprehensive understanding of the challenges faced and the strategies employed by these individuals. Through increased awareness, dialogue, and collaboration, international attorneys can play a crucial role in supporting LGBTQ+ Muslims in their journey towards acceptance, inclusion, and the preservation of their cultural heritage.

Conclusion: Navigating Homosexualism in the Muslim World: Lessons Learned and the Way Forward

In this book, "Navigating Homosexualism in the Muslim World: Legal Challenges and Advocacy," we have explored the complex and multifaceted issues surrounding homosexuality in Muslim communities. Throughout these chapters, we have delved into the legal challenges faced by LGBTQ+ individuals, discussed their experiences, and examined the various ways in which advocacy and activism have been instrumental in promoting LGBTQ+ rights in the Muslim world.

One of the key lessons learned from this exploration is the critical importance of intersectionality. LGBTQ+ Muslims not only face discrimination based on their sexual orientation, but they also navigate multiple marginalized identities, such as race, gender, and religion. Recognizing and addressing these intersecting forms of oppression is crucial in advocating for their rights and creating inclusive spaces within Muslim communities.

Another significant lesson is the power of representation and visibility. LGBTQ+ Muslims often struggle with a lack of visibility and acceptance within their communities. By amplifying their voices, sharing their stories, and showcasing positive portrayals in media and arts, we can challenge stereotypes and foster greater understanding and acceptance within Muslim societies.

Support networks are also vital for LGBTQ+ Muslims. Creating safe spaces, both online and offline, where they can connect with others who share similar experiences, provides a sense of belonging and support. These networks can offer guidance, resources, and emotional support to individuals navigating their identities and coming out to their families and communities.

Furthermore, this book has shed light on the role of queer theology and interpretations of Islam. It has shown that there are alternative understandings of Islamic teachings that affirm LGBTQ+ identities. By engaging in critical discussions and challenging traditional interpretations, we can pave the way for a more inclusive and accepting understanding of Islam that embraces LGBTQ+ individuals.

Lastly, we must address the unique challenges faced by LGBTQ+ Muslim refugees, asylum seekers, and diaspora communities. These individuals often face additional layers of discrimination and isolation, both within their host countries and their own communities. Providing support, legal assistance, and culturally sensitive services to these individuals is crucial in ensuring their safety and well-being.

In conclusion, navigating homosexualism in the Muslim world is a complex and evolving process. However, by learning from the experiences shared in this book and by continuing to advocate for LGBTQ+ rights in Muslim communities, we can work towards creating a more inclusive and accepting world for all individuals, regardless of their sexual orientation or religious beliefs. It is through our collective efforts that we can pave the way for a brighter future for LGBTQ+ Muslims and their communities.